Screening of the Scription

Scott Shaw

Buddha Rose Publications

Screening of the Scription
Copyright 2020 By Scott Shaw
www.scottshaw.com
All Rights Reserved

Cover Photographs By Scott Shaw
Copyright © 2020 All Rights Reserved
Rear Cover Photograph of Scott Shaw By Hae Won Shin
Copyright © 2020 All Rights Reserved.

This book contains material protected under International and Federal Copyright Laws and Treaties. Any unauthorized reprint or use of this material is prohibited. No part of this book may be reproduced or transmitted in any form or by any means, electronic or mechanical, including photocopying, recording, or by any information storage and retrieval system without express written permission from the author or publisher.

First Edition 2020

ISBN 10: 1-949251-24-1
ISBN 13: 978-1-949251-24-1

Printed in the United States of America
10 9 8 7 6 5 4 3 2 1

Screening of the Scription

Introduction

The inspiration for poetry comes from an untold number of sources. At the heart of poetry is the poet attempting to convey what is on their mind and what they are feeling in the most artist manner possible.

Poetry is about feeling. Poetry is about expressing. Poetry is about taking the normal order of words, tying them together in a hopefully new and unique manner and presenting them to the eye's of the reader via a method that will draw that reader in and make them encounter a new reality not necessarily their own.

One of my books, *Nirvana in a Nutshell,* was translated into Vietnamese. One day, I came upon it on my computer and decided to grab a passage, copy it, and see what *Google Translate* did with the interpretation. When I did this, it blew my mind. What *Google Translate* provided me with was amazing. It was a collection of words that I could have never dreamed of putting together. Poetry! It was pure poetry!

What I have presented for you in this book is the *Google Translate* version of the Vietnamese edition of my book, *Nirvana in a Nutshell.* It is a page-by-page presentation. I have left it exactly as it was translated with no spelling or punctuation corrections. It was so perfect that there was nothing else that I could do to bring it to any higher level of poetry.

As for the Vietnamese translation of my book, I, of course, wish to thank the translator and the publishing company for releasing it, as it is a very beautiful edition. I do doubt, however, that the words that are presented on these pages are what the translator actual interpreted but, none-the-less, with the help of *Google Translate* here you have a book of pure poetry—poetic words designed to take you, the reader, to the heart of Zen and hopefully remove you from common consciousness, allowing you to encounter *Satori* via the actualization of words I composed, were then translated, and then deciphered by *Google Translate*.

Screening of the Scription

Notification Notification (NIRVANA IN A NUTSHELL OF SCOTT SHAW) Minh Tam Ngoai Giao diversion * * D D I I E E Ä UÄ U P P H H Ö Ö Cell N N G G x x u u a a t b a a û nû n 2 2 0 0 0 0 9 9 * *

* The developer does not hold the rights *
Welcome to the court or under the form of any other form.

Brief introduction _____

SCREENING OF THE SCRIPTION, SCOPT SHAW's "NIRVANA IN A NUTSHELL" expression of SCOTT SHAW, published by Barnes & Noble in 2003. Scott Shaw is one of the top performers, a home teacher, a homeowner and a co-worker. The content of the book has the first and the first 157 times and the final judgment of the past. Helping people recognize that Giap Ngo is a cross has been able to give birth to all perinatal animals, right here, right now. Branding for people who know who can bring you to the right to show you. It is an adultery that you must give yourself to yourself. You are the ultimate goal of every one of you. Want to get started, you have to buy yourself. It is expected that the effective content will be of great benefit to those who want to learn about the Trades, the Costs and the value after this policy review, which is the same thing that you look at. kisses back to play. Nam Moân Sö Shich Thich Ca Ma Ni Niäät. Dieu Phuong

The first sentence _____ As a result, you can enter the person with the email and you will not have to go back to the past, have a clear view of the problem or have not been approved. In general, the severity of the problem in your symptoms occurs so that you can realize the beauty of our skin. Speaking to you, you send the pictures of a flower to the sky with a clear blue sky, the same style and style. Naturally stabilize the area. In the history book, how many people have learned Nienh Baen. There are people from the past who go back to the temple, and how many hours they have to enter the community in the halls of Hi-Malopon. Other people who know how often are doomed, each step begins at the beginning, looking forward to looking at the quality. Tell me, why do we have to go far away when we hear what it is that we have already done. Take away the distance because people are far away.

It is not possible for you to lose your risk, because people have to spread the word it is the last time that people receive the most frequent damage. You are far from home because you know how many people do not have to suffer from misstatement with the right amount of behavior in your adolescents. This is the same time you use this bar. You are known as a counselor. And as a result, the Venerable Thich Ca Ma Ni Ni, has become an extremely popular source of "source of corruption." Attention, desire, brought you far away from your father as a leader. It is not recommended to be displayed. Just because your ability to give you the same amount of information you don't understand is very important, so you have to struggle to find the right answers for you. Please take a little time to get these sites, cancel all visits, get paid again, and you need to pay. You will now be displayed the same place you are. Display Now. This is you. It is you dissertation on this principle.

Moät _____ What has it recommended for you to stay away from the Public? What to do because you are not a monk? What to do because you do not have to pay for it? What to do because you don't feel right? What to do because you are a stranger? Which one do you need to bring in a career? Yes, you have this. Click here. Carry out the procedure. Two _____ What should you say that you have achieved, or are you saying you? If you can get it done, you can scripting language. If you are a reporter, the article will never run at all.

three _____ People try each email to find your Tracking Name: active, councilor, activist from the background, sexual activities, activities in the streets. They slow down the progress of their lives. Me? Because they believe that when they can show the action, they will look for a Friend. But the activities did not correspond to the Neighbors. Display an action to get the results up and running then what else do people believe when they work? If you set a desired goal, they will never want to want anything else. But as soon as they have been started, they return to their support and continue to want to continue with the other projects. Unacceptable action will not be posted. This is you and you need to go back to another country or another event.

Boán _____ It is important for many people to be the most important person to achieve this life expectancy. These practitioners have considered you as a target from many of these past. If the odds are high, all of these things happen, but it does not work. Every drop, even in foreign countries, will be farther away from you. Me? Because when you believe that you can get anything that you don't have, you don't have to pay the same amount of money that you have to pay. you will be right now. Release in the past and your Current Date.

Seasoning _____ Each conversation begins at a later date. Each section of this school will begin to operate without interruption. Our scientists know that there is a lot of activity around us, the word prince is the best for the largest planet, first in a series of online transitions. This transfer number cannot be recognized by the human person. All these conversions or merged with any other process. If there is no association, the place where we call this place will be closed to us immediately. If a transition is unsuccessful, you must also move and proceed on a similar basis that you do not. Because this is a long term practice - this makes it easy for you to recognize that every time there is a risk. As such, it was first hand in the development process of Vu Tru Tru. Because you are one of the experts in this school, each one is for you, although it is most likely to reach the highest and highest levels of the order. kissing. Your message is accepted. Peace of mind, old and new the negative side effects of foreign languages.

Sauu _____ Usually a credit of one or more credits One of the most important ways to measure information is similar. The follow-up training rates are the most popular and rewarding tips and will be rewarded with the most effective tips. If you say it, you don't have any credit. Baûy _____ People go to the Road for a number of reasons Unable to connect. One when there is a tendency to go to the outside they often participate in a special account. Those who enter in one of these sessions, over time, will always work, be respectable, High quality and prestige in the market of the school. The situation with the sun, the glasses, the high quality and the prestige are not in foreign countries. You are less likely and are not present.

Tails _____ Many people who believe that people are talking about it. Why do you need to leave the call? If you have a discussion - is there anything else you need to know? Nine _____ People are looking for a great deal because they keep the yellow light in their lives. This can be shaped like a love, no purpose, no danger and so on. In Vietnam - people don't want to drink. New _____ Sunyata is a language that means no - A problem with the trade can be resolved. Sunyata is considered as the ladder that has been put into the present. However, when Sunyata came to be a desire in this memorial of trust and this plan comes out.

but the way to expect it to be completed, all of the pure wisdom will be gone. Desires and challenges, generally, you are farther from New York. Because of the action you must take, it is not necessary to remove the activity. Give up your desire. Follow these practices. Follow the Terms. Knowing the Kneading. New one _____ When people are exposed to adultery, the general practitioner or the detractors do not have the same tendency or are in a different manner. Believers generally believe that they should kiss together. As soon as the all-encompasses, the kiss goes back to the marriage. How we all start we do this - every single person who lives with the rest of their lives in school. Do not lose because you are on the road, but you have the right to trust other people.

Every important person in these services is like this. No one kisses or fuss. When you think you have understood - please understand that you do not understand anything. This can be done, but it does not work. Know, but don't say anything. This is a final report of Thien. Thirty two _____ When people get into the practice, they expect the recommendations of a higher authority. It is common to look for a Guru or a Pure Sisters to be guided into the path to Nani. If all our headaches are perinatal and all our headaches are impaired. Why does someone have a code? Not everyone else? Do you recommend this person to someone else? Does it have to be because you have money? How many people, smoothly in the oven, are looked like

What is the secret to the following tips that will produce the price? If any person is healthy in science or get the know-how in the past - Make sure you give the secret to you right away. Thirty three _____ You can listen to other people who talk to you. You can be a full-fledged reader. But, if you behave like the code, You have not yet added to the path that has been added to the Ngoai Thuan Ward, you should only follow the path of a certain path. Supporting language skills when you stop acting as a person and will be a personal teacher for yourself. Everyday _____ Those who access the foreign trade or find the teachings of the Old Masters, believe that they will be treated as a communicator. The achievements and completions of the foreign countries have been achieved.

These days, these days are very good. These rules are not available in any of these countries. As a result, our foreign language process cannot be seen. Literature in the room is obeyed, when you don't know or know the mistakes of the country and do not have to look at a problem. Ten minutes _____ This is because you are a very good person, so that people can be more comfortable with each type of character to get it right. "After you have completed this Agreement, you can take steps to control your overall performance and change your settings." If anyone can do this - what about it? Is it possible for a person to be fully married? Is it necessary to say that you will be able to understand the rights of mystery or whether you will cover the general situation?

New model _____ There are many people who brag about the fact that they have been fully accepted and that their health insurance has been improved. The survival of this life. After you enter one person in a group, put a cup of water in it. To see if the lime water in the cup is suitable for steaming? Everyday _____
When people ask for advice: "Is he a trader?" Repayment: "No, just being a normal person is a normal person." "So, does he have to be a Sō?" "No, just a normal person." New offers _____ The path does not have to be a typical message. Spirituality cannot be measured to see whether there is a pattern or height of kissing.

We all do our best - every person wants to know our personal goals. You have a high level of progress, you will receive this tip. Nine out of nine _____ Many people sign up on their path to receive natural charity such as Buddha Ksetra, "Pharaoh". They believe that it is good to be alive when you live in Hanoi at your fingertips. Natural people are aloof. Naturally paid for. Naturally peaceful and peaceful. The return to the current state is naturally occurring. The system is now more popular in nature. However, you can still work through the restoration of the price. You must not spend peace with the peace or peace of all the surrounding areas. Can you only get foreign credit in your bank? No, the foreign prices may not apply to any country.

Twenty-one _____ Do not write words - from how many days we have been from the past of their past, hope that we will get the same treatment with the same conditions. What is the creation? Excessive culprits - we, similar to people, You can only stay full for a limited period of time. You can also write the word if you want to. But are the letters from the alphabet to you more often? Nope. Giving us the help you give to the person. If you fail to do so due to failures, it is like a return to the performance of the world. You have not done this because of a remote connection or a delay in your production.

Twenty-one minutes _____ Your needs are due to the desire you want or not. Because they are a selective choice, this means that you don't need to walk around the house. You can change your needs if you want to. When there is no need - will know what You Are What You Are. Twenty-two _____ Living there should not be a banan. The same date is a set of maximum CPCs for maximum CPC. This means that people want to experience the repetition. The interest is closed to the date that you are currently away.

Twenty-three _____ It is not a security tool (an adversarial tax code) is usually available to be processed at the maximum level. Me? Because it doesn't mean anything. "There are no costs in these situations." Twenty-one months _____ This is a very similar path to the low temperature. However, how much is the Divine Consumption Act has been written to guide the implementation of the guidelines in accordance with the Board of Management. While there is a great deal of separation, but there are many different rates of education. Is the path to Nienh Baieng not fighting each other? This person is now in full control. Is it not known to anyone? Why are there other things?

Because the rules have not worked yet. Supporting the overall development of the New Year - make it possible that anything cannot be achieved. Current deficits. The Government follows all the pathways labeled with your new password. Twenty-one _____ People who live outside the home country BECAUSE Because of the strong performance in these daily lives. I have to work a lot because I have to say how much is a slave. We have to take a lot of tips because of our relationships. If you can give me something else, do something else - one if you are free, do whatever you want ... What do you want to do if you want to be similar to a foreign or national language? No, you should be immediately logged in, as long as you are working.

Twenty-one late _____ Stopped. Go out. Go down to the most popular street you know. Ha tha thuy. Please accept. Look at your love every time. The official review of the legal frameworks of each of these policies is at the highest and lowest rates. This price is now free - if you look like it is now. All your actions, all your issues have been fully restored. All actions and consequences of other people - even though you do not like the messages. Every letter of investment and commissioning is very effective. See the effect when you continue with the price. The corrected payment is now posted as Disclaimer. Twenty-one days _____
People often show that if they are taken outside the country, they will change.

If you have been told, what else is there to know? Will you not need to drink, drink or drink? Will you not need a crib to survive? Will you not need any money or offer to offer each one of your members? Interpretation is similar to that of the transition - about the same. But life is a life - a human being is a human. As for the old fashioned, "Before the foreign season - the end, the country. After the foreign exchange - cleaning, drink water. " Twenty-one time _____ Maya is used to create similar accounts. In order to recognize the free flow every time, every one of these cases is a no-show effect. It just came out because of our exposure. But what does it mean? Why do we believe we are more effective? These people are giving us the opportunity to show how much we have done in foreign countries.

But why should we be outside? Maya only added that if you did not recognize that you were at the same time as an equivalent. Maya is a smoker. The call is the end of the call. The total sum is not the same amount. This is Neighbor and Maya will be your friend. Twenty-nine _____ What is the description? Is it a must that many people don't have to accept someone to receive it? There are many people who receive a lot of messages - the same information as a leader, but after a lot of time to get the wrong information. laàm. It is not necessary for people to give an analogue as a test that is equivalent to a person who has a disability. Please note that this is the point where you will be tested again. What is the distinction that you are making?

Thirty _____ All your tags received are determined by a large list of ads: and your questions, your economic crisis, your experience, experience, your status in any law, and the main situation in the middle of the world, resulting in a small number of phone calls. Acknowledging is not a right. We are just a reward. Extremely unresponsive behavior. Complete integrity in the field of outreach. Please leave and will be notified. Thirty thirty _____ The experience of each other is different. You can be living in the same world, also in a country, also in the same city, even at the same time or in a similar way - our long-lived experience - our rich experience . They have passed through detections.

Ho ho la ho ho. You are playing. As is the case, do you still have a similar number of people? Or are you sure every person is familiar with their personal development? Thirty two _____

In the process, the mind is promoted to return. hit the ground. With centralized file entry into a single site, the site is no longer active. The person we talk to This score makes it possible for an individual to be able to get Maya's (equivalent) and Granny speech test. Very helpful point of view. Help you with your centralized focus on one of the main ways to complete the previous order. You must not be a progressive national law. What you can't determine is what you have in the world.

Thirty-three _____ On the other hand, Ma-de-la-Ma, a religious monk from Ano, had a conglomerate re-established in China, traveling to China. to return to the Catholic Blessed Children's Association in accordance with the recommendations of this day as a Laotian. registered letters. People break out outside the house, rotate look at one symbolically every nine years. Other than a similar nine-year-old process of achieving anything - Is it foreign? Current display effect. If you want to get out of the ordinary one for nine years to take this action, please do the same. Thirty thirty tips _____ What do you like but you don't see it? If you don't like it - take a quick look.

Thirty thirty years _____ One person inspected in the bed and said, "No, I'm not using it." One day looked at the bed and said, "No, I'm not using it." A common dental practitioner, with a slight increase in age, age, adhesion, screening in bedside and backyard, "I'm very nervous." What is the difference? From the age of wisdom, people believe they can have all of them. The word astrology, the spirit of which we are told, is The belief that spiritual experience is a distant memory that people need to find out more, or how much more is done before, can they be done? Hope you can see it through your phone practical. Where are you now, Right Now, where are you now? You are thinking of yourself What is the best way to do that?

Thirty-one-year-old _____ Why do people who work in foreign countries return to work? How many signatures do you have, how do you do it? Because in order to understand you, you need to work out of the way of your life and think about your position. With the out-of-life ways of life, you can enter a similar amount of money. When you receive the corresponding bonus - You will be recognized immediately. Thirty thirty days _____ Many of the most experienced experiences in the past few years have forced us to buy the software. When you are a kid and if you do not like anything, it is often the case that you are having trouble. When you receive an accident, you are blocked from sexual abuse.

Your and your account of the situation that you are not exposed to: your phone, your life, your life, and the like. If you choose these tips for a normal person, you can simply say, "Looks like old" or "You are out of school." But, does it have to be like that or not - accept the warnings? Many people who are self-responding do not work with the same practice in a similar manner. or outside the house for hours. Is it possible to have a child who is physically and emotionally active? If you go out of the mail the people we played with, if you are away from home The remainder has been delayed, you will find a difference between the value of your property - which is determined by a systematic rule of law - a place where it is not allowed to burn out. No law = Not currently enforced.

Thirty thirty-five _____ When you are disabled, it is more effective. When you have to play the game, it is very spicy. How are you going to behave differently from each other in two cases? Thirty nine _____ The cause of the problem is not participation. Consult the results you want. aspiring to the person you desire, Join us to learn more about each other, or get started, or other things with current status. Attendance is attendance. The investigation is a trial that you are entitled to an agreement. The phone - can be used in your country.

Fourty _____ If you switch to the following items at the same time you do not, you will see that you are familiar with the problem: or a torment, love, continental, or foreign exchange. There is a way to make the time out as if it is going on. Acknowledgment and acceptance of the membership in the community. Look around you, look at you like you've never seen it before. When your new bid is finished, your interest will be reset. Disappear nowadays when available.

Four new months _____ Anonymity is an option. The amount of time that will cost you your money so you can not be safe if you want to get out of your way and work. If you want to continue the delay - stop each task. Canceling. Take this to the throne. Do not give your daily love to you. Take a look and look at the fly A beautiful bird moves across the sky. Understand that no one or three of the things you've put in this insecure security may be able to command your security. Make peace of mind - even among those with the greatest security, the foreigner will come to you.

Forty-two _____ Naturally quiet in each of its roots. The district leader with one community does not work. You are currently disabled if you are currently available. Let your account be the same between the most popular and you'll be notified. Forty-three _____ If all of the countries where you use your language are cleared, why do you have to know that people don't have to pay a fee? Because of the years of exposure, people who do not appear to have an estimate of their age. People read, listen to, and believe in information Remember you must be like that. The story is designed for listening - it is not a question experience. The account cannot be downloaded. Now take a letter that you know and you will receive your Notice.

Fourteen _____ Self-Acting is not a Self-Proverb. A hand-done-practice-centralized system focuses on realizing your needs, finding ways to get the same ideas, and finding the same ways. Some of the same characters that are understood are the needs and actions between people who are similar to each other. As such, there is a lot of room when people look for people who are far away from the Nani River. Forty-five _____ At all times, the Shakyamuni Buddha, the first person to look at the disease, get blemished, and die, die and die, and find the best way to find out. . He has traveled to India for the past year as a Sadhu (a wandering neighbor), or a spiritual translator with the hope of returning to his father's freedom. Due to the failure to find out about the end of the year, it was not in the vicinity of one of the Caesar Islands, Ode Trafficking, and the OCCUParity contract. .

Thirty-one days after the afternoon, he went out again. How many people have passed through multiple signings? Is the code like - outside, sinking into the sky and getting out? How many people are there today, days, days, lots of people and even so many years? The code has not been used yet? The path following the Start button is different with each individual. Uncheck the path for your path. Fourteen days later _____

All actions were followed by the first two children on the pathway to achieve the New Year. Arada Kalama has instructed Akimcanya Ayatana, "Experience and experience." Udraka Ramaputra has taught Naiva Samjna Asamjna Ayatana, "Experience and experience with medicine." The majority of these complaints occur in these two days. In addition to outside, I found a great deal for myself, and returned to a new place.

The outside of the community does not have to be foreign. Your foreign score does not have to be the foreign nationality. The foreign cost of each of these individuals Is there a foreigner's worth of marriage? Four new days _____

It is not safe to create a drug. Repeated failures occur in the Neighborhood. Experiencing the ways of his days, he was very successful in his knowledge and returned to his history. Every individual knows. No one else's error can be used by your friends. If you have an account of the foreign record, you will also not find your Dad. Your qualification is when you aim for others There are similar activities with the Adventurer's Interest.

Forty-five days _____ The word "phap" is derived from the origin of Buddhism as Budh, which means "foreign." In the Pali Dharma Sutra, it appears that there are twenty-one things about the Law or the rules before the Law. Twenty-two times before, how many days after this? The proverbial law always works. Cooked nine _____ Adoption of Adequate Superintendence (high-quality tax): 1. Each animal is born under the Industry. 2. Thousands of removals are attendance. 3. It is not possible to get discounted in foreign countries. 4. Foreign prices can be achieved by following the following practices. Disqualification (abruptly deactivated): 1. Disclosure (understood). 2. Unique thinking (thinking). 3. Stroke (no sign). 4. Discretionary (approved). 5. Network (birth color). 6. Mathematics (it is valid).

7. Disclosure (note). 8. Definition (automatically equivalent). Please note ... New year _____ How many of the same words will be done when implementing the Word and Parent Invoice? How many words have you tried to find instead of looking for a reason because your mind is far from the law? in these dates and the slowdown not used Do you have to go to school and do you have to stop or return to the University of New York? New year _____

The tax rate is the value of each individual. The measure is a measure that is sent by one person to a previous path. Extremely beneficial pricing, but non-contractual payments are not foreign exchange;

This is the history of each other. Reduce the size of the Password and can give it a discount. New year two _____ Acquired by the state, it is similarly similar, almost entirely. Were you similar to your vocabulary? No, it was not. This is the end of the day. What will produce the difference between a number and his or her past? When the person in question gets this question, there's no need to go to another one again, and it gets the most out of it. If you haven't gone to anyone - is your birthday?

Twenty-three years old _____ If you want to keep between your mental health and happiness or reoccurence by another person, you must be exposed to the outside of your mouth. Foreigners are always foreign. Another person can make you happy, but they are not friends. Want to buy? A rule that you might want to make fun for you and is available for you to apply. What happens when you don't want to buy it again? It will be where I say it is you. It doesn't work from outside the door of any other person to give you a lot of stimulation. Having fun using one of our sites, you don't need to find your experience outside. In the middle of the year, Father Truong Son will appear. Father Truong is a path to Nienh Baen.

New year _____ The word Zazen means "out of the sky." This is a common word that is used to describe the word outside the government. Outside the river, circle two times. Focus your channel on one point at a time when you work in a neighborhood. Every time, enter, count, "Moät." Everytime enter, exit, "Hai." "Moät, Hai," "Moät, Hai," "Moät, Hai." Do not let you think anything. When a similar term comes into your mind, watch it fly like a beautiful bird from the sky. Repetition, "Moät, Hai," "Moät, Hai," "Moät, Hai." Fifty years old _____ General definition. The definition you develop gives you a safe and focused mind.

With a safe and focused mind, You have a safe and focused mind in mind. Is a safe mind and a focus on the experience of a Newbie? No, a safe and focused mind is only a safe and focused mind. New year sauu _____ People outside Zazen (outside) because of many wrongdoings. Outside to expect to get through - exited. Extraterritorial expectation is experienced - but similar to the past. Disorder because of us - "I can not go outside kiss you. " External activities for transfer - "I have been determined a time As a result, my final status is shown by the It is taught in a series of channels. " Outside school to be considered as a disaster - out of every Is it better to start outside, right? Zazen is not a familiar brand. Zazen is not a success. Zazen is not a talker. Zazen is not a success. Zazen is not a paradigm shift. Zazen is the only one that does not operate at all.

If you want to try Zazen, don't search, In contrast to the competition, and at the most are no thoughts. Because thinking for you wants you to play an important role while going to Russia as the essence of Zazen. you want to buy it if you want. Think and display. Sugar and thinking about "Outside of God." New year _____
When it is determined, people repeat. The semester will be able to determine whether or not they need to be transferred to the world market. Is it normal for some people or even for many hours a day to tell you? If you are a new user Isn't it a joke or something?

New year _____ People outside the file do not think about anything. Every word without thinking is still a similar word. Cooked seasoning _____ Define your choice with foreign language. Me? Because the default allows you to think that you are missing something. to achieve a similar impact - foreign costs. Something can't be similar to your Current Version. You should only be acknowledged when there is no action. This is the best way to complete the process. Click "Action," Turn on "Activate." Deactivate.

New _____ But outside of the community and not in the community. Is there a foreign exchange? New late _____ It is not possible for you to be annoyed by your external hackers for a long time under certain conditions. The practice guidelines for you are finalized. The results are well-documented and rigorous, because they are recommended for you to maintain an accurate control over the performance of your company. The laws and regulations are not essential to you. They are only a form of law and there are long-term laws. Display a number of natural resources. Please enter your input now you see - This Law Now.

New year two _____ An outsider comes to the conclusion and crawl because you cannot prevent these births from occurring. They allow people around the show to become a romantic partner in the community. The default is to make your mind work, not to kiss. This is to clear your mind of desire. How do you proceed to the same day? You are currently resourced from our account. This lets you enjoy your mind and you will not need to find this secure search using these official polices. The default is to show, not to drop anything. Thirty-three years old _____ A person is in a hurry to add someone to his trade. A number will allow you to add to your account. A lot of people know how to add it to the screen.

A manager or manager to add your own calculations. A scientist to add to your experiment. Yes, how do you add it to your Home Premium? New year _____ The long-term event was a success in the past years of experience. Me? Because people know the ways around. You know - nothing ever again. When nothing is new, there are no more negative experiences and experiences. Definition is a familiar experience. Because it is a familiar experience, after the implementation of these stages, we focus on the same number of times, so that we can achieve the same results. This is due to the fact that people do not think it is possible to treat foreign languages - or confine themselves in an experience that is well experienced. No specific habit is required. It may be new to start outside.

Do you have a situation so you can try it again? Do you allow yourself to become familiar with the experience behind the common rules? This is your choice. The default is your choice. Do this as you will choose. New year _____ You must not be a "me" person. As a result, there are so many people who sign up through the search to find Noodles but they are not approved. You cannot want to be Wanted. Admission is attendance. You can not decide by following the Notice. It is not possible to work. You are not able to use the Control Panel. As the letter is highly advanced. You cannot ask for a Refund. As the parameters are corrupt. You will have, when you are not. The negative effect will be reached in the Current.

New late _____ Can you find a way to find out if you have analogies? New October _____ "You" can never get to Party. Because "You" is a part of your mindset. Thinking Thinking Thinking Again. The General Definition is a manifestation of analogy. Take a look at Nieat Baen. And it will play with you. New year _____ What are you? Do you have to write your name that it will leave and after and will it cover? You must be your mind without spending money tips and advice to change people Or not?

Are you still a spiritual person, you have to download all of the same foreign images and study? Or is it a steaming beam of energy that you haven't heard yet? If you do not see, how do you know it? It is not necessary to believe that there are other people who know that there is a problem that cannot be fully enforced in you, which is first of all. When you can look at your "I", there is no data available. Look at the picture above "I" and you will be back to the New York. Newly ripe _____ All this, The most effective word The largest polluting activity in a region. You also vibrate this function. The former pilgrims who gave this name to this title are "Prana." Chinese people call it "Chi."

Look around you, The culpability of the feature in each one appears in your view. Look at your location. The subject of screenwriting is the same, the management of the country, the cool image of the sun, the effect of a lamp, The movement of vehicles passing. Every item, created by someone or not, starting with this strategy. Remove your vibrations. Log in to the field knife. This is OK. Thirty one _____

Stop playing! Right now, you're now on display. Don't worry about the transition - just stop now! Look around you. Look at each one as you first get it first. Take this time and take a look at the things around you, so that you will find yourself seeing the same days again.

Look at your knowledge and look closely at the distance of the platform to get the most out of these issues. From the file menu to begin, you will first start. I repeat myself to recognize this problem right now and here. You will be thrilled to receive this recognition. New now _____ Many people believe that something is unique and unique to the world. If you can get out of school work, you will be able to get back to work and your family needs. handing over to the headers. Life is a life. It is an effective use of both the performance and the relationship. You are currently showing the time something is wrong important and unique right now - because you're doing the work you're doing. When you are doing the test you are doing, the time transfer a full range of operations.

Save the documents. Free of all attendance. And it shows what is known - to generate a variety of natural resources. Thirty two _____ With the passage of time, Nie is a part of the race. For foreign countries, your country is also one place. The same thing is important - the difference is that. Thinking about this now ... Thirty three _____ A person who believes in treating the times as much as a contest and is as good as a product. If you are away from your body, you will not be able to dissolve all of them, because you will be exposed to all the issues that are important. How is the time-consuming period an interesting event when you like it? How is it always a good thing when you like it in the same way you do? Love being on the law?

This is how to change your life if you're on the go. See each situation as a guide that shows your trail on the road to Nani. Once upon a time _____ The total cost is similar to the purchase date. No longer want to buy anything. The cause is not necessarily urgent. Once upon a time _____ Those who have confidence in their contention prefer to discuss the value of accounting, distribution, judging and evaluation of their jobs - giving them the highest and lowest rates. Put it in Thanh Tinh. People who are not internationally competitive. Because people who do not have foreign language skills only. At the same time, people who do not have to be a foreigner have good faith in it.

Thirty new days _____ The developer does not want to get rich, discretion, fame, love foreign language. Wanting to eat, Nieat Baung will quickly go to the audience. Thirty thirty days _____ Chö Ku in Japanese You mean "No". Ku brand name will be discovered: If you think you are in possession, you are never recommended. Ku is the title of Nani. Give me thirty days _____ It is not possible to understand Ku (Not). It is impossible to define Ku. There are no signs that can be done To recommend for you to take the Ku Ku.

So, what is Ku? Ku also corresponds to Thien. Unable to set a score like this. Cannot enter the new number. Unable to confirm. However, Ku is the closest to Nani Give up all your thoughts. Missing your brand name. Please cancel your definition. Unrecognized cleaning up. And Ku will become the main author. Thirty nine
_____ Ku (Khong) is the treasurer of Thien. You know that you often think that every one is like this. You can think about yourself. You can simulate how you are now. You can try to make a definition of the Version. But if you think about your Dad, you don't understand the Dad and Dad. Ku is voiced, no longer think about anything. Without thinking about anything, you're a Party.

I was told _____ Most people live between their lives in a kind of medical condition. From the born law to the past, go from one of these tips to the next, most of the time. When the life of the past passed, they asked: "Where did you go?" Ku (Not) must be a medical assistant. Ku is a long-time receiver, This is achieved by a similar process with Taam Khong. What is the password? Buo thaem credit. Why do you have to pay from the credit card? Because the information before you go into similar information. Believing is similar to anything you think you know or know. Thinking that there is no reason to see Complaint. It is recognized that Vo-Nem received no equivalent. Voam is the place where you are accepted.

I was told about it _____ There are some caveats appear to be similar to the end of the spectrum. The people who excelled in renunciation, the decision, the courts, and the rest of the transparency. When they are not started, they are disdainful to receive and treat the case. What will happen if there is no follow-up on anything? If you don't want to want anything, Will anyone have to play because it has not been initiated? Complete it. Show now. And you like the bottom. When you try the same device again, Your Note will be available. I invited you two _____ Thinking bouts of wisdom produce. Circumstances are generated by participation.

Join the trail of activities. Action activities that produce Industry. Incorporation, law: What do you plant? You will close it. Ku (Non) Interpretation for you An Occupation is an action, The action is created by participation, Attendance from the source. This is far away. Search for Ku. I was announced on November 3 _____ Since birth we have been reunited to continue to the world, our thinking, our exceptions and our emotions. Characteristics and activities provide us with a number of criteria. Do you like it? How do you do it? Items that do not have to be Done are not. Love is not a ban.

I promised to post _____ Some parents will have a very high medical record to calculate the taxable income of their children. However, the instructions cannot be transmitted again. You will know that you can enjoy yourself. When you think you have understood it, you are They don't know anything. When you calculate your account, you typically do not want people to want your headset, then you will know nothing to know. Ku (Not) is the only way you know it. Tend to open _____ You can crawl by going outside or you can still be yourself. If you let yourself crawl with the exception of your control, you will see that all of your errors will be reversed. What does your control do? Lastly.

What is in your control? How have you lived? Choose the answer. New article _____

People spend a lot of time in their lives to judge how much interest they have in each other's lives: where they live, how they live, who they live together with. Many people believe that if they are banned or many of these out-of-control expenses, they can be found to be similar to the current situation and how much they are expected to be. What again. Because of the similarity in the news, they created a level of peace in the conversation and went to life to follow the schedule. When you have your login file back in Anything outside, though, will be the same in foreign countries, so you will be a contest. The competition never coincides with the average. Anything from outside the time is full or full.

However, the receipt of a payment by an international partner may be sufficient and sufficient. Please leave and understand. I am thirty-three days old _____ People are encouraged to give protection to the currently active products, without any deletion to the past. It can happen to the government or to other people. Me? Because of the delay between the costs of the transfer. "I have to check, isn't it?" "Do I need to go, alright?" "I can't crawl to other people, do I?" These tips do not usually show you just to make clear that the things you want to do with all the prices - no need to see who will influence your performance. Your working name has changed to the end of the day. How are you around? What are you doing to get your attendance? How does this work?

If you cannot answer these questions, what are the reasons that you expect to find a Claim? If you are not able to stop when you are in the area, you know about a law or receive a refund. I told you _____ Severe or chronic. There are no generalizations that are not true. The practice is on time as the case of the Experts. Until you are able to increase your Addiction rate, whether it's good or bad, you can't afford to lose money. Me? Because of the opening you enter human time. If there is an operation, there is an operation. People can love you. People can play with you. Banana, same as each other. If you are confined to your employment cycle, whether or not your practice is good, The same behavior is similar to the automatic behavior. This one is similar to the other. Likewise, the cycle will never go anywhere.

Canceling. Show now. Please leave a new time period. Experimental. Interpretation of drugs. I'm ripe for nine _____ Working is a source of life for many people. A life with lots of people can't prevent you from bouncing around. "I have taken a long distance, if I have a pain." As a result, you are well on the way to gaining experience and experience. "I have been all good, if I get along, I get good results. " If this is not the case, you do want to do it as a fire. Prohibition is not a road that is written in Vietnam. Working as a road has a good reputation. Do not stick to the skin. Improve the relationship between human and human health, and look at people's health and well-being.

These are the results of the results. What you expect will be free, not around. No, you do not know the same thing as you. Nineteen _____ The number of people who received the money first. As a matter of fact, the person who focuses on each of the questions in the search is to find out what the cause is. You have roughly equal amount of money, "Why me?" People often come to see Occupational Disorders. "Were things happening because when I was done?" "Could it be because I was acting like someone?" Or, "What happened? I don't crawl like this! " You can look around the crib to find out why. You can find the duplication rules for the warning. Or, you can accept the end of the world, what things have to go out, and continue the process. Do you think that you will be sold abroad?

Nineteen new _____ Generic terms are created with respect. These tips give rise to the creation. The tips for each issue occur. Each case was created by Industry. If you do not have the similarity in order to give birth to a test result you do not have any performance problems. Therefore, people will not be affected by the symptoms and you do not have to work with birth control. In the month, each day you will be progressively similar. There is no similarity, there is nothing new to be created. When no new jobs are created, no New Job will be created. When there is no New Individuals, you are on your own. You are on the safe side, the school will be as safe as it is. You do not need to create an account to display it. Ninety-nine _____ People evaluate the effectiveness of the Food Marketing Act with their local authorities.

You can follow what you want and get paid. This is done. You can search and search. This also ends. You can say, "I don't need anything and I don't want anything or anyone." Eliminate. Because all of these are included in the tour, you are interested in every reason. Leaving out the items that you want is the first step to be completed. General Mushin, "Voam Taam." Voam is the best place to search for you. Ninety-nine _____ Mushin no Shin, "Food addiction." This practice has a proven track record. It is common for food to be eaten. The general information shows that there are some most common complaints.

The automatic extraction process takes place at the lowest, minimum, or equivalent rate. You confine yourself to your account is that you confine yourself in your email. In the middle of the day, you look at the end of this day; but this is not allowed, but you can not, but the people you can't control are, and the things you have to do, because the results are justified. Unload all of the audio files. Join the tour. Ninety nine months _____ The same word automatically identifies the child on your child's path. Me? Because every word is trustworthy. The word citation results in an obsession with false and false opinions. Sudden and wrong words appear to produce contention. "I know. You are not sure. " "My path is to start because my experiences and judgments have been like this. This means your path is wrong. "

Similar terms never go to the same language. There is no similarity, no conflict. No conflict, the road was closed to Hanoi is now showing. Ninety-nine years later _____ As shown in Mushin, "Voam Taam", you should be sure whether or not you are wrong. You do not save any data or errors that a number has been shown. You are currently visible, so you are available. The current promotion system, you have been successfully opened. Ninety-nine years later _____ Ushin no Shin, "The taste of food is stimulated." With a few ads, you want the first items you want, the strategies you want to buy. You calculated, you specify, You must save a method to set the desired value.

This is a note about the date. The current payment schedule is that you will have achieved the amount you want to expect in a lot, you will also be at risk, because there is a problem. There is a delay in the severity of disability and attendance. With focus on login, Life must meet the needs of both nature and nature. There are no personalities, returns from the chartered school, because the participants cannot be explained. With focus on you, You will never leave your account. By clicking on it, you can get something that you think you want, but you won't be able to find foreign language. Foreign policy cannot be found in one of the main categories of care for the government. Please leave. Ninety nine days _____ It is impossible to think about it. Thoughters may think about it. People thinking that they can just try to read Voam Taam. But, Voam Taam is only visible in you.

Unsubscribe the terms and conditions and will start to search for Voam immediately. Nineteen years old _____ In Mushin (Voam Taam), there is no fighting. Me? Because you want to order every month according to the principle. You are not overwhelmed by the path of your natural human health education. In Mushin, similarities about yourself and the things that you crave cannot be met. end of this contract. Mushin is deadly. Look at yourself. Define all your attendance. When you first review the process you will be taken to the next level of performance. Let us go away from you, dissolve a number of natural objects in space. When there is no attendance, you do not need to create anything. You will return to the beginning of every inspection. As a result, you can now see Mushin.

Nine nine _____ You were born. You live. Then you come here. Your remainder returns to our full position during the transition from law to law. As a result, you do not want to stop playing. If I am only the weakest, why do you have to put so much importance on serving your needs? Remove the dust and will stop using the Neighbors. One piece _____ Once your message is available, you will not be able to use the computer. A trailing path is a kind of mistake. It prompts you to enter a manual. The path you write, but it is you who must go. Are you currently on a Regional Road or Are you merging with Hanoi?

One more thing _____ Have a check if you want to compete. There are people who want to send you, do you, lose your marriage, and immediately follow up with you. To do this, they can take action on what is being done for them. If you are participating in the match, they are already out of practice, because they have been submitted to the campaign. If you are competing, you are falling out, because you have been trying to get rid of the costs of people and people. There are no guidelines, there are no people, no Experiences. Please leave. An additional two _____ What if one of your ads have been removed? If you participate in a competition and determine whether your competition is losing?

The campaign ends up as a result of the campaign. These points are full. Model names, list names, normal performance of operations. How does one campaign bring a healthy dose when people experience pain? There are no warnings. No warnings are complete. One more question _____ The price between you can: start with one another, competing with each other, desire, on the same day, but it is your choice if you want to visit the community. In addition to the current performance of non-foreign brands, this allows them to compete with their policies. To avoid adversity, and they will turn to you to search for peace. When they do this,

Do not give up anything, do not do anything, because if not for anything, there is no need to be repeated. They will be learning from your school and will use it as much as you do. When the time is up, the teacher will continue the process. An additional payment _____ Aam and thunder. If you have to think about data see if you can do it. easy or no, as you are already on average. The average is the lowest natural level. It is understandable that you and the school also have a similar general overview. What does it mean for an average person? When it is not understood that the average is a program natural language of each game. This suggests that people have to take action to adjust each and every action. Do you think, in every one of these cases, there are some open spaces for people? Undertake more peace and peace of mind at our disposal. Your text is like this.

One more year _____ Aura and a coherence of the properties of natural resources. I am this one, you are the other. I am right, you are wrong. I'm a daddy, you're a daddy. I am white, you are black. Missing risk created life. Fault created into Occupation. The source does not generate foreign costs. Break out the risk. Treat yourself as a traffic correspondent with each email. Click to update the date. And you will go to Industry.

A questionnaire _____ If you are interested in Community Assistance. Good and far All of these are your tips and views. If safe and sound, wrong and wrong to enter, Now you need to get rid of your identity as a person who is not familiar with you. This is only one, the most possible. One more question _____ Every person wants to buy People who want to cover. People want to be successful, but only when people know it is natural. Allow people to enter a certain account or This keeps one character from each other known. You generally have the price of the gift, but don't know it. Prices are also the same as your price, which is your term.

Once you have liked your foreign language, you can not get to know it. How do you stay away from being eager to see your favorite color? Best tip: It is not recommended that people know whether you are foreign or not. A questionnaire _____ If you enter the window one hour at a time, contact the shortest time, With the hope that it will be achieved in foreign countries, You will be clear all the time. Don't know or tell the time. One more cooked _____ Refurbished into the environment. You can't see how it looks because you think you know how you will feel and what you will do when you click it. Me?

Because the nicknames "Foreign" have been given to you. Are foreign nationals allowed to study abroad? If you accept the same letter, it is a valid contract. Because they are not foreign, How can you tell your foreigner how? There is a discussion. You now see. Corresponding information. Please use our testing. A new one _____ Extremely effective, but not limited to the past and the most effective. Understand the results. The knowledge is not foreign. The record is, "I know. You don't know. Let me show you. " How this is displayed is similar to the default.

No one can show you about this. You cannot understand this. It does not go away in many cases. A new one _____ Experts receive recommendations from Thinking Manager to calculate the Vo Ta Taam. They have given you the right way to find your way to the bottom. They will give you the secret so that you will be focused on your business. They say you have to be outside, just think that you don't know what else you think or think. you will be using the Parental Control. But the terms and conditions will give birth to a rating. The term of the judge generates a phrase. This word was born in the north. This word bail is born out of luck. Vocabulary play is born high. This tall word is born from the old days. Word term play a similarity. Approaches do not have to be posted in the Neighborhood.

The methods are just simple lines to make the equivalent. How often can you get out without a similar word? If you ask this question, you'll be focusing on the distribution of your code. One hundred and twenty two _____ Some people want to be sold every day. They believe that there are some people who don't understand many people. It is not always possible to know all of the queries. What are the errors? Is it mandatory to recognize individuals who have similar personalities and how they are in the same place? When someone is talking about learning, they only know what they know. What do you know? You can know a lot of things you think you know or know.

One hundred and thirty _____ The price also provides us with a number of numbers of Counselors. Demand must be: big kiss, total kissing, strong kisses, strong kisses, smart kisses, marriage contracts, marriage restrictions. The setting for us a quantity of Counseling and Discrimination: The need is: the kiss bar, start following the rules, By visiting, through a lot of kissing, lots of kissing. The Counselor of the Mind is the Counselor. Interpretation And Prostitution. How often do normal people see who they are or why they are more like them? In Vietnam, people are told that the most common ones are the most common. However, the Foundation has not yet issued

The foreign prices of the country change and change with the similarity of Ta Van and Ta Tri. What you don't know about the Mind. Even the installments of Ta Tri Tri were created by Thien. One more new tip _____ Interesting is the most scientific science. However, because of the characteristic pre-emptiness of medicine, it is the most scientifically determined risk. Because of such similarity, people can tell you what they want and still have the information they follow. Does the same information have to be a foreigner? No, the foreign language is similar, go to your private domain, and ask with your personal knowledge about the site. One hundred and ninety _____ There is a fine chance of flying. There is also a transition of the wild type in the forest. But our parents are our parents, we have a variety of creative ways. Look around to find a pathway with foreign languages that are safe for people. You are now. Disregard your points and shortcomings. Please accept your birth control. And the foreigner must find another place. A new sample _____ Is this allowed for foreign students? A product may work for you on a new phone. A product may be for you new experiences. A product can also be made available to you, which you can trust as a practice. What can be done? What do I have to say is not a good name? If a drug can be given to you, how does it work after your dissolution dissipates - just leave you with the experience? Display Now, when there is nothing else.

A new one day _____ As if you were present in a meeting. Will you describe it? A few new offers _____ Not Available. How many times are you at a certain location, but only to see that you have no problem following the passage of time? How many times have you finished a step without frequenting a new hack? How many people are experiencing something so you know that you are coping with this experience but not having this experience? Because of the longevity of money in the world, many people have a lack of interest in personal life and behavior. what experience in this experience? This has not been a long-term life.

If there is no active interaction with yourself, you have passed away in a new situation, and have been used by anyone who is currently in good health. A new cooked ripe _____ Province. How do you do it? No: "I am an unconventional machine," not necessarily a question. How do you update this law here? Let your mind see if you have the same amount of stress on your body: the ones you do, your father, your father, your fingers, your fingers, yourself, can and your head. After you have finished creating your external code, please use the code in your account. This is a very important and unscrupulous way to do business. Let's see who you are. No one can tell you how to receive them. There are no delays and no errors. Your experience is your experience. If you don't know you, you can't know you. Find out exactly what your first and most successful policies are about.

One two and a half _____ Foreign language users cannot enter the credit card. Foreign students cannot enter the home school. You do not want to delay anything you want in your foreign country. There is no need to make sure that you are satisfied that the price will be overseas. Your foreign currency, Right Now. Log in to this link and use it. One point twenty-one minutes _____ If you want to have a deadline for an inquiry, You can find someone for you to discuss. But, the repetitive length of time is different when asked. different people, each person likes, Click on your personal tags. Enter the order of the payment similarly. Because it is impossible to have a general identity for everyone in a world between positions. If you do not look for questions you will not have to kill people

To prevent an accident, you will return to the ignition area. To prevent bloating, you can start working with your own user interface. You know yourself, you will look at the time between marriage. Because you are the only one who is interested in it. No searchable transgressions, this is a trail in the current state. One and twenty two _____ Each bid has a Thousand Points check: tru truong, life control, human problems, experiences, overseas days. Finding out the Quality Score is the end of the world. The Storing Point is only removed from the exposure. Activities are created by learning, math, math, science, and your study.

Me? Because people want a lot of love. But there are no errors. Any day today that is mathematically or scientifically correct, it may be wrong tomorrow. What are you interested in this day, will come back tomorrow tomorrow. Immediately return the children. Search for Nguoàn Rác. You will find the address of your foreign exchange. One point twenty-three _____ One of the main policies that you will pay for is that you will focus on one of the most well-known areas - either positive or negative. The negative points came. We make sure you have the prices. But the stimulation of the menstrual period, and create for you an audit of your life. But the consequences are not everywhere. At the very beginning of the day, we are now ready to leave. The downs and downs, the downs, the top of the headlines.

How do you do it? Do you cover people with your problems? How will your effects be more similar to your current report? One more twenty-two months _____ Snooping is a spam mail. One when I tried and heard you or are often paid to want or find the same times as you want again. You have to put you on a pattern or is it the top or the bottom of a certain line? But the downsides are not necessary. The only signs are the terms. And the spices will be gone through the night. Optical clarity never lasts longer. Options, Options, Follow one of these steps to find or sign in.

One point twenty-one million _____ Why do you want to cancel the payment? Because you didn't get what you wanted? Because who doesn't behave according to the strategies you want? You can say if you want to. Where will the following remind you? The bottom line is the first, the health, and the additional life. There are no foreign prices. What do you do with a poster? It is important to understand that the birth born by the participants - the desire for anything to be changed. If you're living in your home country, produce the first conversion, People who are not logged in can now be scanned. One and twenty-one years later _____ It is not necessary to control your problems. It is about using the language.

Foreign prices do not have to be far away from your roots. Foreign language is the source of all mail, including your suggestions. Accept the source, you will understand the individual. By managing your account, you will not be able to control any of the main errors that are caused by your abuse. No cow's branch, you are the leader. One step is close to the Current. One point twenty-one days _____ You can add to your common account of human life: the lowest price, tour guide, search, expect, and the downsides you notice are often delayed, if you like this. Or, you can re-create the death penalty of your daily life and the adult language. Playback - you select the option.

One more twenty-one days _____
People produce foreign languages as well. Leading new phone calls. The negative effects of sexual violence are generally high. But supplementation is a negative. Not all at all. With the end of life and death, it is almost always the case. Outreach is far from being effective, because there is no such thing as anything. The term is both full and empty. Are you still having trouble? One two twenty nine _____ If you follow the Disclosure Rule - which opens each message as its location, so you are now entering the URL to see if it is available. "The Little Path of Khaung Nhaat", said. In this situation, you do not have to compete with yourself in the public domain. You do not match the world to the payment methods.

You do whatever you need to do, this is the end of your life, but you don't have enough of the results. There is no adversity, but only for each one. Every day, there is no conflict in you, because you have the same experience in your past and in the past. When there is no dispute. every time you write down the title, it is your approval. Step on the Little Road. One hundred and thirty _____ You can check the price between the documents û around you. You can track the actions of other births. Even if you may be outside and your own bureaucracy, go ahead and give it a conclusion. Or, you may have a medical practice and a successful participation in this strategy. Must I go back to a cave, can it be done overseas? What to do in the end of the trial period will you get to know? You must live in your own home to be a human being. Will the knowledge of human health be more effective?

Disclose all relevant information about the website by any unspecified information. Find out now and you'll know. Show now and you'll be back. One point thirty-one minutes _____ In Japanese, Satori, which says, "Foreign Language". It doesn't work for you. It is all I and then it is unknown. Completely, same as the end of life. This is where it is - on the go, the cycle is full. One point thirty-two _____ You cannot hold Satori (Foreign Language), because there is nothing to throw in. You cannot determine the identity of Satori, because it is not a problem.

Not a part of anything, if it is the most popular template by Thien. One thirty-three _____ You can recall the experience of Satori (Foreign Language), which is your father's name. But if you want to delete the article about Satori, the essence of it will be gone. The essence of this Satori has been so popular in the past few years and many people have played it outside. Satori has not been able to replicate Satori's memory, so that you can know it. When this came out, Satori was no longer there. One quarter of three months _____ People who enter the traditional language space are approved by Satori (Trafficking in Foreign Languages) - they are approved by the Venerable Community. But because of the Satori itself, it is not at full length.

In the middle of it, Identify its identity, The term for is achieved, Only you will never be tested again. Once we stop, we have to find ways. we do not know. Find more ways to cope with Satori's regular discussions. One hundred and thirty percent _____ Some people, just like Satori (Foreign Trade), are a few times the same. The word proverb, critique, collegiality, and critique are very important. It is not possible to use Satori, you can have more space. It is not possible to run Satori, regardless of what you do. Satori is not allowed to appear, although you can see more of it. Satori can only be stunned when it becomes visible.

One and thirty-one years later _____ The Satori (or Foreign Opinion) rating is its latest feature. Check it - then to fill it, Know what is not understood and can be understood and then continue to be good. What will you do after Satori? Save your life. One thirty-three days _____ People want to believe that if they continue to get it ADMINISTRATIVE PRACTICES will never need to be repeated. This means that all needs and expectations will be taken into account. Your needs and expectations are your choice. If you have needs and expect the detector, we will use it. You have a lot of time to hit your ads. Is this the reason why the Correction is detected. The detector detects the sugar level. The roads are ceased to grow.

With very few responses, the post has been delayed. Start advising you what to worry about. In the same way, your profile will be displayed every time and so you will be closed. At the end of the call, you can stop the search and return to the survey. When you have reached the polling point, you will be smoothly saved on your network. Understanding this is an exception. One hundred and thirty percent _____ If you are able to attend the conference you will be worried about in the short term in the course of your stay safely. This is for safety: no education, no worries, no interest, no harm, no pain, no similarity. Dismantling and neglect.

One thirty-nine cooked _____
People like to play in the sun. Adopting the age of five-year-olds from the University of Ho Chi Minh City and hoping to get married again. Do you want your country or foreign country to buy? One new payment _____ What are some people who tell them what to do? Most people are annoying people to talk to to successfully return to the medical and health fields. If you do not know what to expect in your account who are you? People who live outside their home do not have any symptoms. In foreign countries, and you will get the credit of your foreign credit. When important, the importance of your account shows how important it is, because your current risk will be an exception to your health care.

One additional payment _____
You can go outside for a lot of time if you want to be comfortable. You need to enter in one of these channels so that you do not have to pay the same amount of daily traffic. The city and the capital have been automatically transformed into a traditional street path. But what are the words that we have not shown? What are the facts that come out of it except that they are due to a variety of causes of anxiety? The name of the currency group. The deal cannot be considered foreign. On the same day as the trend of physical exclusion. A search for safety in a row. But how much can you find abroad? Look out for foreign languages in the life of your life, and you will be able to find the essence of the New Year's Day, where you can live and in every one. even in jobs you don't want.

One point passed on two _____
What do you get if you don't get rid of the call? You will not have to negotiate with issues in your work. You will not have to start with these mandates that lead to your actions. But how will you live here? Who will give you the name? Who will give you the payment? Do you believe that the order is not available at the time that you will be provided with each email based on your needs?   One   quarter   passed   three _____ The person who likes to pass a lot of time to guess a good life. But like this What will it be done for? Attendance No hazards and nuances. The past days of the re-election to judge the expectations of foreign ownership. But this will work What do I do? Only you are not sure if you have not been successful, or have not had a professional experience to meet your condition.

The two headlines are different, but they are generally results. Adequate taxation, which is the amount of equity. Sugar diversion. Go to Nontang. One new payment on the whole _____ Given your experience, you can see how it works again, It is not possible to know the Location. Just because in a number of business experiences, people often suffer from a pro-social crisis, like, do I need to start? Just because there are a number of people on the stage, the person you believe is a foreign investor, like the head start? Who is most helpful for this: How do you follow the daily requirement and the frequency or number of people on your account to give you? There are no life forms. There are no survivors. You don't have any meaning at all.

Who produced the experiences? Counters. Who favors crests? Individuals. What is the most likely to do? One new payment was renewed _____ But how do mathematicians care about who we look at with code? What are the initial and health risks? If you do not care about the person How I look at myself, I have tried to make myself aware of the other people in the past. It is not a foreign language. Making the order is simply a monk. One hundred and ninety new items _____ Follow the Kinds of Activity button Listening to it as a special script. But when the War ended, the lives ended in the whole.

The life of the race, Nienhi plays. You are a living experience. Does the person with general impairment think about it? One more quarterly _____ A lot of you don't have to be a Knowledge Manager. Many people who enter the city live if one day is very well known for some of the things that they can do. Research brings knowledge back. But knowledge cannot be considered foreign. The exaggerated relationship with knowledge. This article, Please note this tip. One piece of new payment _____ There is no National Tradition. You cannot give it to you. You need to know yourself.

One more cooked nine _____ An account can only be distributed to you at the maximum of all the reports and knowledge of the account. You are the one who has to find our Self-Learned to speak. One year later _____ Follow the steps to set. What do you have to do to get the job done? The first step is to start You can then understand the second test. One year later _____

Now you are currently here, not the same word is going out.

One year twenty-two years _____
In the Vietnamese language, the current meaning is "Summary," when you are someone who is not available at all. Back in the day when you thought about it, skip to the definition. Income is not fully available in the country. Who do you think you are. In the past, and you're going to be around. One year thirteen years _____ Samsara is the constant birthplace of birth and birth Pregnancy is bound to be different, with no negative results when a small number of people go to the New Year. The Law of the Taot Law is the danger of a crime Foreigners, who passed this time, will continue to postpone the delay, until they are closed. The birth of a newborn man. Parental activism - the path of success in New York.

One year of payment _____ As a rule of thumb, many of the laws that make law, law, and employment laws lead to a new life. or Completely follow the rules that will be processed. Do these have been tested for the essence of Thien or not? It is not a tradition. Actual, direct, and direct practice with Thien. This is a perfect analogy with Tri Tueä and Cao Tri Adopted. Experiments for the birth of a newborn. Does foreign practice depend on rituals? Are foreign countries suspicious? Does foreign language training follow the same program schedule? No, this is not the case. But what are the most common ones? must follow the laws, regulations, and operational procedures that are expected from each step of the process. Many people don't know this. Please re-enter the deadline. This is a trick. The price of foreign exchange.

One year later _____ One of the main reasons for the recent death in Ba Ria-Vung Tau is because many people have difficulty in developing their language skills. "I am on the way back to the world, there is no problem that you have to do it." Why do people have to be depressed? Why am I not allowed to have fun? Abandon the wrong symbols. On the other hand, it helps to preserve the image of the monastic life through the practice of its members, which is expected to be achieved in a number of foreign languages, They love fun. Non-technical knowledge. The people who create language critics don't need to know Nani is the only person who has a negative effect on Nani's. Click on the essence of the New York and return to your home.

One time when you lost your password, you took a different time. Foreign language report, a different kind of people. One year later _____ No one can give you Current. It is a product that you give yourself to yourself.

THE ZEN

www.ingramcontent.com/pod-product-compliance
Lightning Source LLC
Chambersburg PA
CBHW062116080426
42734CB00012B/2881